Dr Michael M. Gruneberg, designer and writer of the Gruneberg Linkword Language Courses, is widely regarded as an international expert on memory improvement. A Senior Lecturer in Psychology at University College, Swansea, he has published a large number of articles in scientific journals, as well as a number of well-known books on the application of memory research. He has also lectured widely in both the UK and the USA and given keynote addresses to several international scientific conferences. In 1988 he provided the original script for, and appeared in, *The Magic of Memory*, a programme in the BBC television QED series which illustrated many memory techniques, including his own Linkword Method, and he recently acted as principal scientific consultant for a major BBC 1 series on memory.

Since it was first published in 1987, the Linkword system has been both highly successful and widely acclaimed and Linkword books are now published throughout the world. Dr Gruneberg works with highly qualified language experts to produce Linkword books which teach you not only **what** to learn, but **how to remember what you have learned**, more quickly and more enjoyably than you ever imagined!

Gabriel C. Jacobs BA, PhD,
the language consultant for this book, is a
Senior Lecturer in the School of European
Languages at Swansea University. He has
been involved for some time in the practical
application of language.

Also by Dr Michael M. Gruneberg

LINKWORD LANGUAGE SYSTEM: SPANISH

LINKWORD: FRENCH IN A DAY
LINKWORD LANGUAGE SYSTEM: FRENCH
LINKWORD LANGUAGE SYSTEM: FURTHER FRENCH
LINKWORD LANGUAGE SYSTEM: GERMAN
LINKWORD LANGUAGE SYSTEM: ITALIAN
LINKWORD LANGUAGE SYSTEM: GREEK
LINKWORD LANGUAGE SYSTEM: PORTUGUESE
(with Dr G. C. Jacobs)

and published by Corgi Books

LINKWORD

SPANISH
IN A DAY

Dr Michael M. Gruneberg

Language Consultant
Dr Gabriel C. Jacobs

CORGI BOOKS

LINKWORD: SPANISH IN A DAY

A CORGI BOOK : 0 552 14247 6

First publication in Great Britain

PRINTING HISTORY
Corgi edition published 1994

Set in 9pt Linotype New Century Schoolbook by
Phoenix Typesetting, Ilkley, West Yorkshire.

Corgi Books are published by Transworld Publishers Ltd,
61–63 Uxbridge Road, Ealing, London W5 5SA,
in Australia by Transworld Publishers (Australia) Pty Ltd,
15–25 Helles Avenue, Moorebank, NSW 2170,
and in New Zealand by Transworld Publishers (NZ) Ltd,
3 William Pickering Drive, Albany, Auckland.

Reproduced, printed and bound in Great Britain by
Cox & Wyman Ltd, Reading, Berks.

Contents

Foreword

This book is designed to get you to pick up, **in a single day,** an extensive targeted vocabulary which will enable you to communicate in useful situations you are likely to meet in Spain, such as in the restaurant, at the hotel, travelling, shopping, in emergencies and so on. It is ideal, therefore, if you have to be in Spain tomorrow or next week on holiday or business, or for the student who wants to acquire an extensive vocabulary rapidly. You can even learn a useful amount on the plane!

Why then is learning so quick and easy? Because Linkword courses are unique in **not only teaching you what to learn, but how to remember what you learn.** This is done through the use of images which make you link the English word to another word which sounds like the Spanish word you want to remember. For example, the Spanish word for Rice is Arroz. You are asked to picture **arrows** landing in your rice.

Over fifty studies published in scientific journals have shown this method to be far superior to ordinary methods of learning. In one study the number of foreign words remembered increased from 28% to 88% using this method. What is more, the method works for those who are good at language learning and those who are poor at it. Even more important, a number of studies show that the great majority of people find it more **fun** learning this way.

This book concentrates on teaching useful nouns, although other helpful words are included. This is because if you are beginning a language nouns are all-important for communication. If you are in a restaurant for example, and can say 'Bill please!', you will be presented with the bill. If you just say 'I want' you won't get anything! You will be amazed at how much difference a knowledge of the contents of this book will make to your enjoyment of your holiday or trip abroad and to overcoming the feeling of isolation you often get when you don't understand the language of the country you are visiting. Anyone who has ever used a phrase book will know how difficult they are to use, and how useful it is to know the words one needs, instead of trying to look them up. This book allows you to be your own mental phrase book!

When you have finished this book you can go on to learn even more Spanish by using Linkword Spanish, a more advanced Spanish language course, and its accompanying audio tape which will help to improve your pronunciation.

How to use Linkword

1] You will be presented with words like this:
The Spanish for CAT is GATO
Imagine a CAT eating a lovely GATEAU
What you do is to imagine this picture in your mind's eye as vividly as possible.

2] After you have read the image you should think about it in your mind's eye for about 10 seconds before moving on to the next word. If you do not spend enough time thinking about the image it will not stick in your memory as well as it should.

3] Sometimes the word in Spanish and in English is the same or very similar. For example, the Spanish for 'taxi' is 'taxi'. When this happens you will be asked to associate the word in some way with a bullfighter.

For example:
Imagine a taxi filled with bullfighters.
Whenever bullfighters come to mind, therefore, you will know the word is the same or similar in both English and Spanish.

4] **PRONUNCIATION**
The approximate pronunciation of words is given in brackets after the word is presented for the first time.

Don't worry too much about these pronunciations to begin with. The approximate pronunciations given in brackets will allow you to be understood.

5] ACCENTS

When you see the accent Ñ you should pronounce it NY

For example: The Spanish for TOMORROW is MAÑANA

MANYANA is the way the word is pronounced.

When you see an acute accent (´) on a letter you should emphasize the syllable with the accented letter in it.

For example: The Spanish for MOUSE is RATÓN

RAT*ON* is the way the word is pronounced with the emphasis on the ON (*not RAT*ON)

IMPORTANT NOTES

Don't worry if you don't get all the words correct the first time you go through the book. No-one can expect to get all the words right first time. Don't worry about what you can't remember, think of all the words you do remember! Only after you have reached the end of the book should you go back to learn any words you have forgotten.

You can carry on learning until you feel tired. However, if you begin to feel tired, you must stop and take a break.

FOOD AND DRINK WORDS

THINK OF EACH IMAGE IN YOUR MIND'S EYE FOR ABOUT TEN SECONDS. FOR EXAMPLE, THE SPANISH FOR *SOUP* IS *SOPA*. IMAGINE IN YOUR MIND'S EYE A *SOUP* WHICH TASTES LIKE *SOAP*.

NOTE: THE WORD IN BRACKETS ON THE RIGHT HAND SIDE OF THE PAGE IS THE WAY THE WORD IS PRONOUNCED.

O   The Spanish for SOUP is SOPA   (SOPA)
     Imagine a soup which tastes like SOAP

O   The Spanish for RICE is ARROZ   (ARROTH)
     Imagine someone shooting ARROWS which
     land on your plate of rice.

O   The Spanish for ONION is CEBOLLA   (THEBOLYA)
     Imagine one onion turning to another and
     saying 'THEY BOIL YOU in this place.'

O   The Spanish for TOMATO is TOMATE   (TOMATAY)
     Imagine throwing TOMATOES at a bullfighter.
     * Remember that every time you see a bullfighter the word
       is the same or similar in English and Spanish

O   The Spanish for CHEESE is QUESO   (KESO)
     Imagine a CASE O' cheese

O   The Spanish for EGG is HUEVO   (HOO EVO)
     Imagine you give a WAVE O to someone who
     throws eggs at you.

O   The Spanish for WATER is AGUA   (AGWA)
     Imagine an AQUADUCT bringing water to your hotel.

O   The Spanish for SUGAR is AZÚCAR   (ATHOOKAR)
     Imagine stuffing A CIGAR into the sugar bowl.

O   The Spanish for COFFEE is CAFÉ   (KAFAY)
     Imagine drinking coffee in a CAFE.

1

YOU CAN WRITE YOUR ANSWERS IN, BUT COVER UP THE
RIGHT-HAND PAGE BEFORE GIVING YOUR ANSWERS

○   What is the English for café?   _____

○   What is the English for azúcar?   _____

○   What is the English for agua?   _____

○   What is the English for huevo?   _____

○   What is the English for queso?   _____

○   What is the English for tomate?   _____

○   What is the English for cebolla?   _____

○   What is the English for arroz?   _____

○   What is the English for sopa?   _____

TURN BACK FOR THE ANSWERS

YOU CAN WRITE YOUR ANSWERS IN, BUT COVER UP THE
LEFT-HAND PAGE BEFORE GIVING YOUR ANSWERS

O   What is the Spanish for coffee?   _____

O   What is the Spanish for sugar?   _____

O   What is the Spanish for water?   _____

O   What is the Spanish for egg?   _____

O   What is the Spanish for cheese?   _____

O   What is the Spanish for tomato?   _____

O   What is the Spanish for onion?   _____

O   What is the Spanish for rice?   _____

O   What is the Spanish for soup?   _____

TURN BACK FOR THE ANSWERS

CLOTHES

THINK OF EACH IMAGE IN YOUR MIND'S EYE FOR ABOUT TEN SECONDS.

○ The Spanish for HAT is SOMBRERO   (SOMBRERO)
Imagine being given a large SOMBRERO
when you ask for a hat.

○ The Spanish for SHOE is ZAPATO   (THAPATO)
Imagine a shoe on THE PATIO.

○ The Spanish for TROUSERS is   (PANTALONES)
PANTALONES
Imagine wearing baggy PANTALOONS for trousers.

○ The Spanish for SKIRT is FALDA   (FALDA)
Imagine you FOLD A skirt away.

○ The Spanish for BLOUSE is BLUSA   (BLOOSA)
Imagine a BLUE blouse.

○ The Spanish for SHIRT is CAMISA   (KAMEESA)
Imagine shouting 'COME HERE SIR and get your shirt'.

○ The Spanish for DRESS is VESTIDO   (VESTEEDO)
Imagine telling a little girl after putting her
dress on that she should wear a VESTI TOO!

○ The Spanish for BATHING TRUNKS is   (BANYADOR)
BAÑADOR
Imagine you BANG THE DOOR with your bathing trunks.

O   What is the English for bañador?   _____

O   What is the English for vestido?   _____

O   What is the English for camisa?   _____

O   What is the English for blusa?   _____

O   What is the English for falda?   _____

O   What is the English for pantalones?   _____

O   What is the English for zapato?   _____

O   What is the English for sombrero?   _____

YOU CAN WRITE YOUR ANSWERS IN

O   What is the Spanish for bathing trunks?   _____

O   What is the Spanish for dress?   _____

O   What is the Spanish for shirt?   _____

O   What is the Spanish for blouse?   _____

O   What is the Spanish for skirt?   _____

O   What is the Spanish for trousers?   _____

O   What is the Spanish for shoe?   _____

O   What is the Spanish for hat?   _____

TURN BACK FOR THE ANSWERS

FURNITURE AND FITTINGS

THINK OF EACH IMAGE IN YOUR MIND'S EYE FOR ABOUT TEN SECONDS.

○   The Spanish for BED is CAMA   (KAMA)
    Imagine a CAMEL lying on your bed.

○   The Spanish for TABLE is MESA   (MESA)
    Imagine a MESSY table.

○   The Spanish for CHAIR is SILLA   (SEELYA)
    Imagine a girl called CELIA sitting down on a large chair.

○   The Spanish for CURTAIN is CORTINA   (KORTEENA)
    Imagine you CONCERTINA your curtains
    when you open them.

○   The Spanish for CUPBOARD is ARMARIO   (ARMARYO)
    Imagine you keep an ARMOURY of weapons
    in your cupboard.

○   The Spanish for CLOCK is RELOJ   (RELOH)
    Imagine RELOADING a clock.

○   The Spanish for SHELF is ESTANTE   (ESTANTAY)
    Imagine putting up INSTANT shelving.

○   The Spanish for DRAWER is CAJÓN   (KAHON)
    Imagine a CAR HORN sounds every time you
    open your drawer.

YOU CAN WRITE YOUR ANSWERS IN, BUT COVER UP THE
RIGHT-HAND PAGE BEFORE GIVING YOUR ANSWERS

○   What is the English for cajón?   _____

○   What is the English for estante?   _____

○   What is the English for reloj?   _____

○   What is the English for armario?   _____

○   What is the English for cortina?   _____

○   What is the English for silla?   _____

○   What is the English for mesa?   _____

○   What is the English for cama?   _____

TURN BACK FOR THE ANSWERS

YOU CAN WRITE YOUR ANSWERS IN, BUT COVER UP THE
LEFT-HAND PAGE BEFORE GIVING YOUR ANSWERS

○   What is the Spanish for drawer?   _____

○   What is the Spanish for shelf?   _____

○   What is the Spanish for clock?   _____

○   What is the Spanish for cupboard?   _____

○   What is the Spanish for curtain?   _____

○   What is the Spanish for chair?   _____

○   What is the Spanish for table?   _____

○   What is the Spanish for bed?   _____

TURN BACK FOR THE ANSWERS

MORE FOOD AND DRINK WORDS

THINK OF EACH IMAGE IN YOUR MIND'S EYE FOR ABOUT TEN SECONDS.

○   The Spanish for BREAD is PAN   (PAN)
Imagine loaves of bread stuffed in a PAN.

○   The Spanish for MEAT is CARNE   (KARNAY)
Imagine CARNIVORES eating meat.

○   The Spanish for POTATO is PATATA   (PATATA)
Imagine throwing POTATOES at a bullfighter.

○   The Spanish for WINE is VINO   (VEENO)
Imagine a German saying 'VE KNOW
what a good wine it is.'

○   The Spanish for MILK is LECHE   (LECHAY)
Imagine LEECHES in the milk.

○   The Spanish for BEER is CERVEZA   (THERVETHA)
Imagine demanding SERVICE for your beer in a pub.

○   The Spanish for PEAR is PERA   (PERA)
Imagine buying a PAIR A pears.

○   The Spanish for CAKE is PASTEL   (PASTEL)
Imagine a PASTEL coloured cake.

YOU CAN WRITE YOUR ANSWERS IN, BUT COVER UP THE LEFT-HAND PAGE BEFORE GIVING YOUR ANSWERS

O   What is the English for pastel?   _____

O   What is the English for pera?   _____

O   What is the English for cerveza?   _____

O   What is the English for leche?   _____

O   What is the English for vino?   _____

O   What is the English for patata?   _____

O   What is the English for carne?   _____

O   What is the English for pan?   _____

YOU CAN WRITE YOUR ANSWERS IN

O   What is the Spanish for cake?   _____

O   What is the Spanish for pear?   _____

O   What is the Spanish for beer?   _____

O   What is the Spanish for milk?   _____

O   What is the Spanish for wine?   _____

O   What is the Spanish for potato?   _____

O   What is the Spanish for meat?   _____

O   What is the Spanish for bread?   _____

TURN BACK FOR THE ANSWERS

EMERGENCY WORDS

THINK OF EACH IMAGE IN YOUR MIND'S EYE FOR ABOUT TEN SECONDS.

○ The Spanish for HOSPITAL is HOSPITAL   (OSPEETAL)
Imagine a bullfighter being carted off to HOSPITAL.

○ The Spanish for BANDAGE is VENDA   (VENDA)
Imagine you BEND A bandage
backwards and forwards to get it OFF.

○ The Spanish for AMBULANCE is   (AMBULANTHYA)
AMBULANCIA
Imagine a bullfighter being loaded into an AMBULANCE.

○ The Spanish for ACCIDENT is   (AKTHEEDENTAY)
ACCIDENTE
Imagine a bullfighter in a nasty ACCIDENT.

○ The Spanish for THIEF is LADRÓN   (LADRON)
Imagine a thief disappearing down the
street with a LADDER ON his back.

○ The Spanish for FIRE is FUEGO   (FOO EGO)
Imagine telling the hotel manager
'IF WE GO there will be a fire.'

○ The Spanish for HELP is AYUDA   (AYOODA)
Imagine shouting 'HEY YOU THERE, help!'

○ The Spanish for TELEPHONE is
TELÉFONO   (TELEFONO)
Imagine a bullfighter using a TELEPHONE.

13

YOU CAN WRITE YOUR ANSWERS IN, BUT COVER UP THE RIGHT-HAND PAGE BEFORE GIVING YOUR ANSWERS

O   What is the English for teléfono?   _____

O   What is the English for ayuda?   _____

O   What is the English for fuego?   _____

O   What is the English for ladrón?   _____

O   What is the English for accidente?   _____

O   What is the English for ambulancia?   _____

O   What is the English for venda?   _____

O   What is the English for hospital?   _____

TURN BACK FOR THE ANSWERS

YOU CAN WRITE YOUR ANSWERS IN, BUT COVER UP THE
LEFT-HAND PAGE BEFORE GIVING YOUR ANSWERS

O   What is the Spanish for telephone?   _____

O   What is the Spanish for help?   _____

O   What is the Spanish for fire?   _____

O   What is the Spanish for thief?   _____

O   What is the Spanish for accident?   _____

O   What is the Spanish for ambulance?   _____

O   What is the Spanish for bandage?   _____

O   What is the Spanish for hospital?   _____

TURN BACK FOR THE ANSWERS

NOW TEST YOURSELF

What is the Spanish for

1] BREAD...
2] WINE ....
3] MILK..
4] HAT..
5] SKIRT ....
6] BED..
7] TABLE ....
8] DRAWER ....
9] SOUP ....
10] RICE ....
11] ONION...
12] SUGAR..
13] BANDAGE....................................
14] THIEF...
15] TELEPHONE ....

What is the English for

1] PATATA ....
2] CERVEZA ....
3] ZAPATO................................
4] BLUSA ....
5] VESTIDO ....
6] BAÑADOR ....
7] CORTINA..............................
8] ARMARIO ....
9] ESTANTE ....
10] QUESO.................................
11] AGUA ....
12] TOMATE ....
13] CAFÉ....................................
14] FUEGO..................................
15] AYUDA.................................

Do not worry about the spelling at this stage.

THE ANSWERS ARE ON PAGE 18

THE ANSWERS ARE

1]	PAN	1]	POTATO
2]	VINO	2]	BEER
3]	LECHE	3]	SHOE
4]	SOMBRERO	4]	BLOUSE
5]	FALDA	5]	DRESS
6]	CAMA	6]	BATHING TRUNKS
7]	MESA	7]	CURTAIN
8]	CAJÓN	8]	CUPBOARD
9]	SOPA	9]	SHELF
10]	ARROZ	10]	CHEESE
11]	CEBOLLA	11]	WATER
12]	AZÚCAR	12]	TOMATO
13]	VENDA	13]	COFFEE
14]	LADRÓN	14]	FIRE
15]	TELÉFONO	15]	HELP

Count yourself correct if the word *sounds* like the Spanish word you are looking for. If you scored 15/30 you have now learned more than 20 words. If you managed to translate all the words, you can assume you have learned all the words given up till now, i.e. 40 words.

RESTAURANT WORDS

THINK OF EACH IMAGE IN YOUR MIND'S EYE FOR ABOUT TEN SECONDS.

O   The Spanish for RESTAURANT is RESTAURANTE (RESTA OORANTAY)
Imagine a bullfighter in your RESTAURANT.

O   The Spanish for WAITRESS is CAMARERA (KAMARERA)
Imagine a waitress with a CAMERA slung around her neck.

O   The Spanish for CUP is TAZA (TATHA)
Imagine a cup with a TASSLE dangling from the handle.

O   The Spanish for BILL is CUENTA (KWENTA)
Imagine your friend WENT Away when it came to paying the bill.

O   The Spanish for MENU is MENÚ (MENOO)
Imagine a bullfighter studying the MENU.

O   The Spanish for PLATE is PLATO (PLATO)
Imagine you climb a mountain and reach a PLATEAU all covered with white plates.

O   The Spanish for KNIFE is CUCHILLO (KOOCHEELYO)
Imagine someone with a knife saying 'With this I COULD CHILL YOU.'

O   The Spanish for FORK is TENEDOR (TENEDOR)
Imagine prodding a piece of meat with a fork to make sure it is TENDER.

O   The Spanish for TABLECLOTH is MANTEL (MANTEL)
Imagine a tablecloth on the MANTELpiece.

O   The Spanish for BOTTLE is BOTELLA (BOTELYA)
Imagine throwing a BOTTLE at a bullfighter.

YOU CAN WRITE YOUR ANSWERS IN, BUT COVER UP THE
RIGHT-HAND PAGE BEFORE GIVING YOUR ANSWERS

○　　What is the English for botella?　　　_____

○　　What is the English for mantel?　　　_____

○　　What is the English for tenedor?　　　_____

○　　What is the English for cuchillo?　　　_____

○　　What is the English for plato?　　　_____

○　　What is the English for menú?　　　_____

○　　What is the English for cuenta?　　　_____

○　　What is the English for taza?　　　_____

○　　What is the English for camarera?　　　_____

○　　What is the English for restaurante?　　　_____

TURN BACK FOR THE ANSWERS

YOU CAN WRITE YOUR ANSWERS IN, BUT COVER UP THE
LEFT-HAND PAGE BEFORE GIVING YOUR ANSWERS

○   What is the Spanish for bottle?   _____

○   What is the Spanish for tablecloth?   _____

○   What is the Spanish for fork?   _____

○   What is the Spanish for knife?   _____

○   What is the Spanish for plate?   _____

○   What is the Spanish for menu?   _____

○   What is the Spanish for bill?   _____

○   What is the Spanish for cup?   _____

○   What is the Spanish for waitress?   _____

○   What is the Spanish for restaurant?   _____

TURN BACK FOR THE ANSWERS

AT THE DOCTOR'S

THINK OF EACH IMAGE IN YOUR MIND'S EYE FOR ABOUT TEN SECONDS.

O   The Spanish for PAIN is DOLOR   (DOLOR)
      Imagine being given a DOLLAR to make your pain go away.

O   The Spanish for ILL is ENFERMO   (ENFERMO)
      Imagine being ill and INFIRM.

O   The Spanish for COUGH is TOS   (TOS)
      Imagine you cough in the middle of TOSSING
      a coin, and drop the coin.

O   The Spanish for ARM is BRAZO   (BRATHO)
      Imagine BRASS bracelets wrapped around your arm.

O   The Spanish for EYE is OJO   (OHO)
      Imagine the doctor saying 'OH HO!' as he
      pokes you in the eye.

O   The Spanish for FACE is CARA   (KARA)
      Imagine your face looking as if a CAR HAD hit it.

O   The Spanish for HAND is MANO   (MANO)
      Imagine dropping someone's hand down a MANHOLE.

O   The Spanish for SKIN is PIEL   (PEE EL)
      Imagine your skin beginning to PEEL in the sun.

O   The Spanish for BLOOD is SANGRE   (SANGRAY)
      Imagine being SO ANGRY that you draw blood.

O   The Spanish for MOUTH is BOCA   (BOKA)
      Imagine A POKER sticking out of someone's mouth.

YOU CAN WRITE YOUR ANSWERS IN, BUT COVER UP THE
LEFT-HAND PAGE BEFORE GIVING YOUR ANSWERS

O   What is the English for boca?   _____

O   What is the English for sangre?   _____

O   What is the English for piel?   _____

O   What is the English for mano?   _____

O   What is the English for cara?   _____

O   What is the English for ojo?   _____

O   What is the English for brazo?   _____

O   What is the English for tos?   _____

O   What is the English for enfermo?   _____

O   What is the English for dolor?   _____

YOU CAN WRITE YOUR ANSWERS IN

○   What is the Spanish for mouth?   _____

○   What is the Spanish for blood?   _____

○   What is the Spanish for skin?   _____

○   What is the Spanish for hand?   _____

○   What is the Spanish for face?   _____

○   What is the Spanish for eye?   _____

○   What is the Spanish for arm?   _____

○   What is the Spanish for cough?   _____

○   What is the Spanish for ill?   _____

○   What is the Spanish for pain?   _____

TURN BACK FOR THE ANSWERS

FAMILY WORDS

THINK OF EACH IMAGE IN YOUR MIND'S EYE FOR ABOUT TEN SECONDS.

○ The Spanish for FATHER is PADRE   (PADRAY)
Imagine your father dressed up as a PADRE.

○ The Spanish for MOTHER is MADRE   (MADRAY)
Imagine your mother very MAD at you.

○ The Spanish for BROTHER is HERMANO   (ERMANO)
Imagine your brother is a HAIRY MAN, OH!

○ The Spanish for SISTER is HERMANA   (ERMANA)
Imagine your sister loves a HAIRY MAN, AH!
(But the word ends in 'A' not 'O'.)

○ The Spanish for HUSBAND is MARIDO   (MAREEDO)
Imagine your husband is MARRIED!

○ The Spanish for WIFE is MUJER   (MOOHER)
Imagine your wife is dressed in a MOHAIR coat.

○ The Spanish for BOY is MUCHACHO   (MOOCHACHO)
Imagine a boy who MOOS when a CHAT-
SHOW comes on: MOO-CHA-CHO.

○ The Spanish for GIRL is MUCHACHA   (MOOCHACHA)
Imagine a girl who MOOS, then does a
CHA-CHA: MOO-CHA-CHA.

○ The Spanish for SON is HIJO   (EEHO)
Imagine your son going EE-HO, just like a donkey.

○ The Spanish for DAUGHTER is HIJA   (EEHA)
Imagine your daughter sounding like a
female donkey, with an 'a' at the end: EE-HA.

YOU CAN WRITE YOUR ANSWERS IN, BUT COVER UP THE
RIGHT-HAND PAGE BEFORE GIVING YOUR ANSWERS

O   What is the English for hija?   _____

O   What is the English for hijo?   _____

O   What is the English for muchacha?   _____

O   What is the English for muchacho?   _____

O   What is the English for mujer?   _____

O   What is the English for marido?   _____

O   What is the English for hermana?   _____

O   What is the English for hermano?   _____

O   What is the English for madre?   _____

O   What is the English for padre?   _____

TURN BACK FOR THE ANSWERS

YOU CAN WRITE YOUR ANSWERS IN, BUT COVER UP THE
LEFT-HAND PAGE BEFORE GIVING YOUR ANSWERS

O   What is the Spanish for daughter?   _____

O   What is the Spanish for son?   _____

O   What is the Spanish for girl?   _____

O   What is the Spanish for boy?   _____

O   What is the Spanish for wife?   _____

O   What is the Spanish for husband?   _____

O   What is the Spanish for sister?   _____

O   What is the Spanish for brother?   _____

O   What is the Spanish for mother?   _____

O   What is the Spanish for father?   _____

TURN BACK FOR THE ANSWERS

TRAVELLING WORDS

THINK OF EACH IMAGE IN YOUR MIND'S EYE FOR ABOUT TEN SECONDS.

○ The Spanish for BOAT is BARCO   (BARKO)
  Imagine a dog BARKING as you embark on a boat.

○ The Spanish for CAR is COCHE   (KOCHAY)
  Imagine your car is converted into an
  old-fashioned COACH.

○ The Spanish for BUS is AUTOBÚS   (AOOTOBOOS)
  Imagine A BUS filled with bullfighters.

○ The Spanish for TRAIN is TREN   (TREN)
  Imagine bullfighters leaning out of TRAIN carriages.

○ The Spanish for GARAGE is GARAJE   (GARAHAY)
  Imagine a bullfighter serving petrol on the
  forecourt of a GARAGE.

○ The Spanish for PETROL is GASOLINA   (GASOLEENA)
  Imagine filling your car with GAS instead of petrol.

○ The Spanish for OIL is ACEITE   (ATHAY EETAY)
  Imagine oil being so ACIDY that it burns
  a hole when you drop some.

○ The Spanish for PUNCTURE is PINCHAZO
  Imagine when a lady bends down to   (PEENCHATHO)
  inspect a puncture you PINCH HER,
  THOUGH we're not saying where!

○ The Spanish for WHEEL is RUEDA   (ROO EDA)
  Imagine little wheels appearing on a RADAR screen.

○ The Spanish for JACK is GATO   (GATO)
  Imagine using a sponge GATEAU as a jack.

O   What is the English for gato?   _____

O   What is the English for rueda?   _____

O   What is the English for pinchazo?   _____

O   What is the English for aceite?   _____

O   What is the English for gasolina?   _____

O   What is the English for garaje?   _____

O   What is the English for tren?   _____

O   What is the English for autobús?   _____

O   What is the English for coche?   _____

O   What is the English for barco?   _____

YOU CAN WRITE YOUR ANSWERS IN

○   What is the Spanish for jack?   _____

○   What is the Spanish for wheel?   _____

○   What is the Spanish for puncture?   _____

○   What is the Spanish for oil?   _____

○   What is the Spanish for petrol?   _____

○   What is the Spanish for garage?   _____

○   What is the Spanish for train?   _____

○   What is the Spanish for bus?   _____

○   What is the Spanish for car?   _____

○   What is the Spanish for boat?   _____

TURN BACK FOR THE ANSWERS

ARRIVING AT YOUR DESTINATION

THINK OF EACH IMAGE IN YOUR MIND'S EYE FOR ABOUT TEN SECONDS.

O   The Spanish for PASSPORT is PASAPORTE
Imagine a bullfighter stamping your   (PASAPORTAY)
PASSPORT when you arrive in Spain.

O   The Spanish for SUITCASE is MALETA   (MALETA)
Imagine MY LETTER is in your suitcase.

O   The Spanish for CUSTOMS is ADUANA   (ADWANA)
Imagine going through the customs saying
'ADD ONE. Add two', etc.

O   The Spanish for TOILET is RETRETE   (RETRETAY)
Imagine RETREATING to the toilet.

O   The Spanish for TICKET is BILLETE   (BEELYETAY)
Imagine thinking 'I will BE LATE if I don't find my tickets.'

O   The Spanish for DANGER is PELIGRO   (PELEEGRO)
Imagine someone shouting 'Danger, don't
eat that, it will make your BELLY GROW.'

O   The Spanish for GENTLEMEN is SEÑORES
Imagine a number of SENIOR men   (SENYORAYS)
entering the gentlemen's toilet.

O   The Spanish for LADIES is SEÑORAS   (SENYORAS)
Imagine a number of SENIOR ladies
entering the ladies' toilet.

O   The Spanish for ENTRANCE is ENTRADA   (ENTRADA)
Imagine a bullfighter ENTERING A bullring.

O   The Spanish for EXIT is SALIDA   (SALEEDA)
Imagine a SALAD spread all over the exit to your hotel.

YOU CAN WRITE YOUR ANSWERS IN, BUT COVER UP THE
RIGHT-HAND PAGE BEFORE GIVING YOUR ANSWERS

O   What is the English for salida?   _____

O   What is the English for entrada?   _____

O   What is the English for señoras?   _____

O   What is the English for señores?   _____

O   What is the English for peligro?   _____

O   What is the English for billete?   _____

O   What is the English for retrete?   _____

O   What is the English for aduana?   _____

O   What is the English for maleta?   _____

O   What is the English for pasaporte?   _____

TURN BACK FOR THE ANSWERS

YOU CAN WRITE YOUR ANSWERS IN, BUT COVER UP THE
LEFT-HAND PAGE BEFORE GIVING YOUR ANSWERS

O   What is the Spanish for exit?   _____

O   What is the Spanish for entrance?   _____

O   What is the Spanish for ladies?   _____

O   What is the Spanish for gentlemen?   _____

O   What is the Spanish for danger?   _____

O   What is the Spanish for ticket?   _____

O   What is the Spanish for toilet?   _____

O   What is the Spanish for customs?   _____

O   What is the Spanish for suitcase?   _____

O   What is the Spanish for passport?   _____

TURN BACK FOR THE ANSWERS

NUMBERS

THINK OF EACH IMAGE IN YOUR MIND'S EYE FOR ABOUT TEN SECONDS.

○ The Spanish for ONE is UNO   (OONO)
    Imagine YOU KNOW ONE.

○ The Spanish for TWO is DOS   (DOS)
    Imagine you TOSS TWO coins in the air.

○ The Spanish for THREE is TRES   (TRES)
    Imagine THREE TREES in front of you.

○ The Spanish for FOUR is CUATRO   (KWATRO)
    Imagine drinking FOUR bottles of COINTREAU.

○ The Spanish for FIVE is CINCO   (THEENKO)
    Imagine being bathed in the SINK O when you
    were FIVE years old.

○ The Spanish for SIX is SEIS   (SAY EES)
    Imagine someone who SAYS SIX.

○ The Spanish for SEVEN is SIETE   (SEE ETAY)
    Imagine your SETTEE has seen SEVEN deadly sins.

○ The Spanish for EIGHT is OCHO   (OCHO)
    Imagine the number EIGHT painted in OCHRE.

○ The Spanish for NINE is NUEVE   (NOO EVAY)
    Imagine dialling 999 for the NAVY.

○ The Spanish for ZERO is CERO   (THERO)
    Imagine ZERO is NOTHING to a bullfighter.

YOU CAN WRITE YOUR ANSWERS IN, BUT COVER UP THE
LEFT-HAND PAGE BEFORE GIVING YOUR ANSWERS

○   What is the English for uno?   _____

○   What is the English for dos?   _____

○   What is the English for tres?   _____

○   What is the English for cuatro?   _____

○   What is the English for cinco?   _____

○   What is the English for seis?   _____

○   What is the English for siete?   _____

○   What is the English for ocho?   _____

○   What is the English for nueve?   _____

○   What is the English for cero?   _____

YOU CAN WRITE YOUR ANSWERS IN

○   What is the Spanish for one?   _____

○   What is the Spanish for two?   _____

○   What is the Spanish for three?   _____

○   What is the Spanish for four?   _____

○   What is the Spanish for five?   _____

○   What is the Spanish for six?   _____

○   What is the Spanish for seven?   _____

○   What is the Spanish for eight?   _____

○   What is the Spanish for nine?   _____

○   What is the Spanish for zero?   _____

TURN BACK FOR THE ANSWERS

NOW TEST YOURSELF

What is the Spanish for   *What is the English for*

1]	BREAD	1]	CEBOLLA ....
2]	WINE	2]	ZAPATO ....
3]	TROUSERS	3]	CAMISA ....
4]	BED	4]	MESA ....
5]	WATER	5]	PERA ....
6]	HOSPITAL	6]	ACCIDENTE ....
7]	PLATE	7]	CUENTA ....
8]	FORK	8]	MANTEL ....
9]	PAIN	9]	BRAZO ....
10]	COUGH	10]	PIEL ....
11]	FATHER	11]	SANGRE ....
12]	HUSBAND	12]	HERMANO ....
13]	BOAT	13]	HIJO ....
14]	PUNCTURE	14]	COCHE ....
15]	SUITCASE	15]	RUEDA ....
16]	TOILET	16]	GATO ....
17]	EXIT	17]	ADUANA ....
18]	THREE	18]	PELIGRO ....
19]	FIVE	19]	ENTRADA ....
20]	ZERO	20]	NUEVE ....

Do not worry about the spelling at this stage.

THE ANSWERS ARE ON PAGE 38

THE ANSWERS ARE

1] PAN	1] ONION
2] VINO	2] SHOE
3] PANTALONES	3] SHIRT
4] CAMA	4] TABLE
5] AGUA	5] PEAR
6] HOSPITAL	6] ACCIDENT
7] PLATO	7] BILL
8] TENEDOR	8] TABLECLOTH
9] DOLOR	9] ARM
10] TOS	10] SKIN
11] PADRE	11] BLOOD
12] MARIDO	12] BROTHER
13] BARCO	13] SON
14] PINCHAZO	14] CAR
15] MALETA	15] WHEEL
16] RETRETE	16] JACK
17] SALIDA	17] CUSTOMS
18] TRES	18] DANGER
19] CINCO	19] ENTRANCE
20] CERO	20] NINE

Since you have now covered 100 words, if your score on this test is over 20/40 you have learned 50 words. If your score is 40/40 you have learned 100 words. Do not worry about spelling errors at this stage of learning.

GENERALLY USEFUL WORDS

THINK OF EACH IMAGE IN YOUR MIND'S EYE FOR ABOUT TEN SECONDS.

○ The Spanish for DOCTOR is MÉDICO   (MEDEEKO)
Imagine your doctor with bottles of MEDICINE.

○ The Spanish for DENTIST is DENTISTA
Imagine a bullfighter at the DENTIST'S.   (DENTEESTA)

○ The Spanish for LAWYER is ABOGADO   (ABOGADO)
Imagine a lawyer eating an AVOCADO
pear in the middle of the defence of his client.

○ The Spanish for POLICE is POLICÍA   (POLEETHEE A)
Imagine the POLICE arresting a bullfighter.

○ The Spanish for BANK is BANCO   (BANKO)
Imagine your BANK filled with bullfighters.

○ The Spanish for HOTEL is HOTEL   (OTEL)
Imagine a bullfighter's convention at your HOTEL.

○ The Spanish for POST OFFICE is CORREO   (KORREO)
Imagine a post office in KOREA, with
Korean signs outside.

○ The Spanish for CAMPING SITE is CAMPING
Imagine bullfighters CAMPING at a   (CAMPEENG)
camping site.

YOU CAN WRITE YOUR ANSWERS IN, BUT COVER UP THE
RIGHT-HAND PAGE BEFORE GIVING YOUR ANSWERS

○   What is the English for camping?   _____

○   What is the English for correo?   _____

○   What is the English for hotel?   _____

○   What is the English for banco?   _____

○   What is the English for policía?   _____

○   What is the English for abogado?   _____

○   What is the English for dentista?   _____

○   What is the English for médico?   _____

TURN BACK FOR THE ANSWERS

O   What is the Spanish for camping site?   _____

O   What is the Spanish for post office?   _____

O   What is the Spanish for hotel?   _____

O   What is the Spanish for bank?   _____

O   What is the Spanish for police?   _____

O   What is the Spanish for lawyer?   _____

O   What is the Spanish for dentist?   _____

O   What is the Spanish for doctor?   _____

TURN BACK FOR THE ANSWERS

ON THE BEACH

THINK OF EACH IMAGE IN YOUR MIND'S EYE FOR ABOUT TEN SECONDS.

O   The Spanish for BEACH is PLAYA   (PLA YA)
Imagine you PLAY A game on the beach.

O   The Spanish for SAND is ARENA   (ARENA)
Imagine clowns in a circus ARENA
throwing sand at each other.

O   The Spanish for DECKCHAIR is HAMACA   (AMAKA)
Imagine a HAMMOCK slung between two deckchairs.

O   The Spanish for PICNIC is MERIENDA   (MEREE ENDA)
Imagine your picnic coming to a MERRY END,
possibly because people have drunk too much..

O   The Spanish for SUN is SOL   (SOL)
Imagine SAUL in the Bible, staring at the sun.

O   The Spanish for COLD is FRÍO   (FREE O)
Imagine being FREEzing cold.

O   The Spanish for HEAT is CALOR   (KALOR)
Imagine using CALOR gas to heat something up.

O   The Spanish for SEA is MAR   (MAR)
Imagine yelling 'MA! get me out of the sea.'

YOU CAN WRITE YOUR ANSWERS IN, BUT COVER UP THE
LEFT-HAND PAGE BEFORE GIVING YOUR ANSWERS

O   What is the English for mar?   _____

O   What is the English for calor?   _____

O   What is the English for frío?   _____

O   What is the English for sol?   _____

O   What is the English for merienda?   _____

O   What is the English for hamaca?   _____

O   What is the English for arena?   _____

O   What is the English for playa?   _____

YOU CAN WRITE YOUR ANSWERS IN

○   What is the Spanish for sea?   _____

○   What is the Spanish for heat?   _____

○   What is the Spanish for cold?   _____

○   What is the Spanish for sun?   _____

○   What is the Spanish for picnic?   _____

○   What is the Spanish for deckchair?   _____

○   What is the Spanish for sand?   _____

○   What is the Spanish for beach?   _____

TURN BACK FOR THE ANSWERS

MORE TRAVELLING WORDS

THINK OF EACH IMAGE IN YOUR MIND'S EYE FOR ABOUT TEN SECONDS.

O   The Spanish for TYRE is NEUMÁTICO (NE OOMATEEKO)
     Imagine blowing up a PNEUMATIC tyre.

O   The Spanish for EXHAUST is ESCAPE   (ESKAPAY)
     Imagine exhaust fumes ESCAPING from a car.

O   The Spanish for KEY is LLAVE   (LYAVAY)
     Imagine that you have left your key in the LAVATORY.

O   The Spanish for ENGINE is MOTOR   (MOTOR)
     Imagine your MOTOR car won't start
     because the engine has broken down.

O   The Spanish for DRIVER is CONDUCTOR
     Imagine the driver of your car   (KONDOOKTOR)
     is a bus CONDUCTOR.

O   The Spanish for FAN is VENTILADOR   (VENTEELADOR)
     Imagine you use a fan for a
     VENTILATOR for your car.

O   The Spanish for SEAT is ASIENTO   (ASEE ENTO)
     Imagine you have to ASCEND TO sit on your seat.

O   The Spanish for TANK is DEPÓSITO   (DEPOSEETO)
     Imagine you DEPOSIT petrol in your tank.

YOU CAN WRITE YOUR ANSWERS IN, BUT COVER UP THE
RIGHT-HAND PAGE BEFORE GIVING YOUR ANSWERS

O   What is the English for depósito?   _____

O   What is the English for asiento?   _____

O   What is the English for ventilador?   _____

O   What is the English for conductor?   _____

O   What is the English for motor?   _____

O   What is the English for llave?   _____

O   What is the English for escape?   _____

O   What is the English for neumático?   _____

TURN BACK FOR THE ANSWERS

**YOU CAN WRITE YOUR ANSWERS IN, BUT COVER UP THE
LEFT-HAND PAGE BEFORE GIVING YOUR ANSWERS**

O   What is the Spanish for tank?   _____

O   What is the Spanish for seat?   _____

O   What is the Spanish for fan?   _____

O   What is the Spanish for driver?   _____

O   What is the Spanish for engine?   _____

O   What is the Spanish for key?   _____

O   What is the Spanish for exhaust?   _____

O   What is the Spanish for tyre?   _____

TURN BACK FOR THE ANSWERS

GENERALLY USEFUL WORDS

THINK OF EACH IMAGE IN YOUR MIND'S EYE FOR ABOUT TEN SECONDS.

○ The Spanish for THANK YOU is GRACIAS   (GRATHYAS)
Imagine someone being GRACIOUS and
saying THANK YOU.

○ The Spanish for PLEASE is POR FAVOR   (POR FAVOR)
Imagine thinking 'PLEASE POUR
FAVOURS in my direction.'

○ The Spanish for SORRY is PERDONE   (PERDONAY)
Imagine saying 'PARDON. I am SORRY.'

○ The Spanish for HELLO is HOLÁ   (OLA)
Imagine saying 'HELLO' to someone who is
practising with a HOOLA-hoop.

○ The Spanish for GOOD-BYE is ADIÓS   (ADYOS)
Imagine thinking 'GOOD-BYE IDIOTS!'

○ The Spanish for ONLY is SOLAMENTE   (SOLAMENTAY)
Imagine thinking 'If ONLY SOLOMON MEANT IT.'

○ The Spanish for VERY is MUY   (MWEE)
Imagine MWE are VERY good at Spanish.

○ The Spanish for YES is SÍ   (SEE)
Imagine answering 'YES. SÍ Señor! Yes Sir.'

○ The Spanish for NO is NO   (NO)
Imagine thinking 'NO! NO! Mr. Bullfighter.'

○ The Spanish for NOT is NO   (NO)
Imagine saying 'No, NOT, NO!'

48

YOU CAN WRITE YOUR ANSWERS IN, BUT COVER UP THE
LEFT-HAND PAGE BEFORE GIVING YOUR ANSWERS

○ What is the English for no?   _____

○ What is the English for sí?   _____

○ What is the English for muy?   _____

○ What is the English for solamente?   _____

○ What is the English for adiós?   _____

○ What is the English for holá?   _____

○ What is the English for perdone?   _____

○ What is the English for por favor?   _____

○ What is the English for gracias?   _____

YOU CAN WRITE YOUR ANSWERS IN

O   What is the Spanish for no or not?   _____

O   What is the Spanish for yes?   _____

O   What is the Spanish for very?   _____

O   What is the Spanish for only?   _____

O   What is the Spanish for goodbye?   _____

O   What is the Spanish for hello?   _____

O   What is the Spanish for sorry?   _____

O   What is the Spanish for please?   _____

O   What is the Spanish for thank you?   _____

TURN BACK FOR THE ANSWERS

MORE FURNITURE AND FITTINGS

THINK OF EACH IMAGE IN YOUR MIND'S EYE FOR ABOUT TEN SECONDS.

○ The Spanish for STAIRS is ESCALERA   (ESKALERA)
   Imagine ESCALATORS in your house instead of stairs.

○ The Spanish for FLOOR is SUELO   (SWELO)
   Imagine a big SWELLING rising up in the floor.

○ The Spanish for WALL is PARED   (PARED)
   Imagine watching a PARADE from the top of a high wall.

○ The Spanish for KITCHEN is COCINA   (KOTHEENA)
   Imagine being COSY IN A kitchen.

○ The Spanish for BEDROOM is DORMITORIO
   Imagine your bedroom has been   (DORMEETORYO)
   turned into a DORMITORY, with lots
   of people sleeping in it.

○ The Spanish for DOOR is PUERTA   (PWERTA)
   Imagine a hotel PORTER opening a door for you.

○ The Spanish for WINDOW is VENTANA   (VENTANA)
   Imagine a German fly that VENT ON A window.

○ The Spanish for GARDEN is JARDÍN   (HARDEEN)
   Imagine someone working HARD IN the garden.

51

YOU CAN WRITE YOUR ANSWERS IN, BUT COVER UP THE RIGHT-HAND PAGE BEFORE GIVING YOUR ANSWERS

O   What is the English for jardín?   _____

O   What is the English for ventana?   _____

O   What is the English for puerta?   _____

O   What is the English for dormitorio?   _____

O   What is the English for cocina?   _____

O   What is the English for pared?   _____

O   What is the English for suelo?   _____

O   What is the English for escalera?   _____

TURN BACK FOR THE ANSWERS

YOU CAN WRITE YOUR ANSWERS IN, BUT COVER UP THE
LEFT-HAND PAGE BEFORE GIVING YOUR ANSWERS

○   What is the Spanish for garden?   _____

○   What is the Spanish for window?   _____

○   What is the Spanish for door?   _____

○   What is the Spanish for bedroom?   _____

○   What is the Spanish for kitchen?   _____

○   What is the Spanish for wall?   _____

○   What is the Spanish for floor?   _____

○   What is the Spanish for stairs?   _____

TURN BACK FOR THE ANSWERS

DAYS OF THE WEEK

THINK OF EACH IMAGE IN YOUR MIND'S EYE FOR ABOUT TEN SECONDS.

○ The Spanish for MONDAY is LUNES (LOONAYS)
Imagine only LOONIES go to work on Monday.

○ The Spanish for TUESDAY is MARTES (MARTAYS)
Imagine you always burn MARTYRS on Tuesdays.

○ The Spanish for WEDNESDAY is MIÉRCOLES
Imagine praying for MIRACLES on (MEE ERCOLAYS)
Wednesday so that the end of the week will come quickly.

○ The Spanish for THURSDAY is JUEVES (HOO EVAYS)
Imagine you WAVE US good-bye on Thursdays.

○ The Spanish for FRIDAY is VIERNES (VEE ERNAYS)
Imagine showing your BARE KNEES
on Friday, to celebrate the end of the week.

○ The Spanish for SATURDAY is SÁBADO (SABADO)
Imagine Saturday is the Jewish SABBATH.

○ The Spanish for SUNDAY is DOMINGO (DOMEENGO)
Imagine you play DOMINOES with your
family on Sunday evening before shunting them off to bed.

YOU CAN WRITE YOUR ANSWERS IN, BUT COVER UP THE
LEFT-HAND PAGE BEFORE GIVING YOUR ANSWERS

O   What is the English for domingo?   _____

O   What is the English for sábado?   _____

O   What is the English for viernes?   _____

O   What is the English for jueves?   _____

O   What is the English for miércoles?   _____

O   What is the English for martes?   _____

O   What is the English for lunes?   _____

YOU CAN WRITE YOUR ANSWERS IN

O   What is the Spanish for Sunday?   _____

O   What is the Spanish for Saturday?   _____

O   What is the Spanish for Friday?   _____

O   What is the Spanish for Thursday?   _____

O   What is the Spanish for Wednesday?   _____

O   What is the Spanish for Tuesday?   _____

O   What is the Spanish for Monday?   _____

TURN BACK FOR THE ANSWERS

MORE FOOD WORDS

THINK OF EACH IMAGE IN YOUR MIND'S EYE FOR ABOUT TEN SECONDS.

O The Spanish for CLAM is ALMEJA   (ALMEHA)
   Imagine saying 'I'LL MAKE US some clam soup.'

O The Spanish for SQUID is CALAMAR   (KALAMAR)
   Imagine its COLOUR MARS the taste of squid.

O The Spanish for PRAWN is GAMBA   (GAMBA)
   Imagine you GAMBLE on a prawn to win a race.

O The Spanish for LOBSTER is LANGOSTA   (LANGOSTA)
   Imagine dropping lobsters from a
   LANCASTER bomber.

O The Spanish for MUSSEL is MEJILLÓN   (MEHILYON)
   Imagine cutting up a MELON and mussels falling out.

O The Spanish for PORK is CERDO   (THERDO)
   Imagine a waiter asking 'CARE TO eat pork?'

O The Spanish for CHOP is CHULETA   (CHULETA)
   Imagine you CHEW LETTERS to stop eating chops.

O The Spanish for FILLET is FILETE   (FILETEH)
   Imagine a bullfighter eating a FILLET steak.

O The Spanish for STEW is ESTOFADO   (ESTOFADO)
   Imagine someone IS TOO FAT OH! to eat big plates of stew.

O The Spanish for SAUSAGE is   (SALCHEECHA)
   SALCHICHA
   Imagine I SHALL TEACH YOU how to eat sausages.

YOU CAN WRITE YOUR ANSWERS IN, BUT COVER UP THE
RIGHT-HAND PAGE BEFORE GIVING YOUR ANSWERS

O   What is the English for almeja?   _____

O   What is the English for calamar?   _____

O   What is the English for gamba?   _____

O   What is the English for langosta?   _____

O   What is the English for mejillón?   _____

O   What is the English for cerdo?   _____

O   What is the English for chuleta?   _____

O   What is the English for filete?   _____

O   What is the English for estofado?   _____

O   What is the English for salchicha?   _____

TURN BACK FOR THE ANSWERS

YOU CAN WRITE YOUR ANSWERS IN, BUT COVER UP THE
LEFT-HAND PAGE BEFORE GIVING YOUR ANSWERS

○   What is the Spanish for sausage?   _____

○   What is the Spanish for stew?   _____

○   What is the Spanish for fillet?   _____

○   What is the Spanish for chop?   _____

○   What is the Spanish for pork?   _____

○   What is the Spanish for mussel?   _____

○   What is the Spanish for lobster?   _____

○   What is the Spanish for prawn?   _____

○   What is the Spanish for squid?   _____

○   What is the Spanish for clam?   _____

TURN BACK FOR THE ANSWERS

QUESTION WORDS AND VERBS

THINK OF EACH IMAGE IN YOUR MIND'S EYE FOR ABOUT TEN SECONDS.

○ The Spanish for WHERE is DÓNDE   (DONDAY)
Imagine asking 'WHERE on earth is DUNDEE?'

○ The Spanish for WHY is POR QUÉ   (POR KAY)
Imagine asking your mother 'WHY PORK for tea again?'

○ The Spanish for HOW is CÓMO   (KOMO)
Imagine asking 'HOW COME?'

○ The Spanish for WHO is QUIÉN   (KEE EN)
Imagine an ignorant person asking 'WHO IS QUEEN?'

○ The Spanish for HOW MUCH is CUÁNTO   (KWANTO)
Imagine asking HOW MUCH it is when you
buy a large QUANTITY.

○ The Spanish for I WANT is QUIERO   (KEE ERO)
Imagine I WANT to QUERY everything.

○ The Spanish for I HAVE is TENGO   (TENGO)
Imagine I HAVE to TANGO.

○ The Spanish for I SPEAK is HABLO   (HABLO)
Imagine every time I SPEAK, I BLOW.

○ The Spanish for I TAKE is TOMO   (TOMO)
Imagine I take a TOMAhawk from your head.

○ The Spanish for I WRITE is ESCRIBO   (ESKREEBO)
Imagine when I WRITE, I SCRIBBLE.

YOU CAN WRITE YOUR ANSWERS IN, BUT COVER UP THE
LEFT-HAND PAGE BEFORE GIVING YOUR ANSWERS

○   What is the English for escribo?   _____

○   What is the English for tomo?   _____

○   What is the English for hablo?   _____

○   What is the English for tengo?   _____

○   What is the English for quiero?   _____

○   What is the English for cuánto?   _____

○   What is the English for quién?   _____

○   What is the English for cómo?   _____

○   What is the English for por qué?   _____

○   What is the English for dónde?   _____

YOU CAN WRITE YOUR ANSWERS IN

○   What is the Spanish for I write?   _____

○   What is the Spanish for I take?   _____

○   What is the Spanish for I speak?   _____

○   What is the Spanish for I have?   _____

○   What is the Spanish for I want?   _____

○   What is the Spanish for how much?   _____

○   What is the Spanish for who?   _____

○   What is the Spanish for how?   _____

○   What is the Spanish for why?   _____

○   What is the Spanish for where?   _____

TURN BACK FOR THE ANSWERS

TIME WORDS

THINK OF EACH IMAGE IN YOUR MIND'S EYE FOR ABOUT TEN SECONDS.

O The Spanish for SECOND is SEGUNDO   (SEGOONDO)
Imagine a bullfighter tapping his feet every SECOND.

O The Spanish for MINUTE is MINUTO   (MEENOOTO)
Imagine a bullfighter killing a bull once a MINUTE.

O The Spanish for HOUR is HORA   (ORA)
Imagine waiting in HORROR for the hour to strike.

O The Spanish for WEEK is SEMANA   (SEMANA)
Imagine going to a SEMINAR once a week.

O The Spanish for MONTH is MES   (MES)
Imagine being in a MESS once a month.

O The Spanish for YEAR is AÑO   (ANYO)
Imagine a year is ANNUAL.

O The Spanish for DAY is DÍA   (DEE A)
Imagine thinking everything is DEAR during the day.

O The Spanish for NIGHT is NOCHE   (NOCHAY)
Imagine NOCTURNAL animals come out at night.

YOU CAN WRITE YOUR ANSWERS IN, BUT COVER UP THE
RIGHT-HAND PAGE BEFORE GIVING YOUR ANSWERS

○   What is the English for noche?   _____

○   What is the English for día?   _____

○   What is the English for año?   _____

○   What is the English for mes?   _____

○   What is the English for semana?   _____

○   What is the English for hora?   _____

○   What is the English for minuto?   _____

○   What is the English for segundo?   _____

TURN BACK FOR THE ANSWERS

64

YOU CAN WRITE YOUR ANSWERS IN, BUT COVER UP THE
LEFT-HAND PAGE BEFORE GIVING YOUR ANSWERS

O   What is the Spanish for night?   _____

O   What is the Spanish for day?   _____

O   What is the Spanish for year?   _____

O   What is the Spanish for month?   _____

O   What is the Spanish for week?   _____

O   What is the Spanish for hour?   _____

O   What is the Spanish for minute?   _____

O   What is the Spanish for second?   _____

TURN BACK FOR THE ANSWERS

GENERALLY USEFUL WORDS

THINK OF EACH IMAGE IN YOUR MIND'S EYE FOR ABOUT TEN SECONDS.

○ The Spanish for FRIEND is AMIGO   (AMEEGO)
Imagine telling my friend that I MAY GO
if he is not more pleasant to me.

○ The Spanish for AFTERNOON is TARDE   (TARDAY)
Imagine being so late and TARDY at
getting up that it is the afternoon before you appear.

○ The Spanish for NUMBER is NUMERO   (NOOMERO)
Imagine someone giving you
NUMEROUS numbers for his telephone number.

○ The Spanish for PAPER is PAPEL   (PAPEL)
Imagine everyone throwing paper during a PAPAL visit.

○ The Spanish for ROOM is   (ABEETATHYON)
HABITACIÓN
Imagine thinking 'This room is not fit
for human HABITATION'.

○ The Spanish for LETTER BOX is BUZÓN   (BOOTHON)
Imagine a BOOTH ON top of a letter box.

○ The Spanish for BATH is BAÑO   (BANYO)
Imagine they BAN YOU from having a bath.

○ The Spanish for MORNING is MAÑANA   (MANYANA)
Imagine greeting a MAN YOU KNOW every morning.

YOU CAN WRITE YOUR ANSWERS IN, BUT COVER UP THE LEFT-HAND PAGE BEFORE GIVING YOUR ANSWERS

O   What is the English for mañana?   _____

O   What is the English for baño?   _____

O   What is the English for buzón?   _____

O   What is the English for habitación?   _____

O   What is the English for papel?   _____

O   What is the English for número?   _____

O   What is the English for tarde?   _____

O   What is the English for amigo?   _____

YOU CAN WRITE YOUR ANSWERS IN

O   What is the Spanish for morning?   _____

O   What is the Spanish for bath?   _____

O   What is the Spanish for letter box?   _____

O   What is the Spanish for room?   _____

O   What is the Spanish for paper?   _____

O   What is the Spanish for number?   _____

O   What is the Spanish for afternoon?   _____

O   What is the Spanish for friend?   _____

TURN BACK FOR THE ANSWERS

GENERALLY USEFUL WORDS

THINK OF EACH IMAGE IN YOUR MIND'S EYE FOR ABOUT TEN SECONDS.

○ The Spanish for CIGARETTE is (THEEGAREELYO)
CIGARILLO
Imagine Spanish cigarettes are like
little CIGARS that make you ILL OH!

○ The Spanish for BREAKFAST is (DESAYOONO)
DESAYUNO
Imagine someone coming up to you in an hotel
and saying 'THEY SAY YOU KNOW when
breakfast is.'

○ The Spanish for LUNCH is COMIDA (KOMEEDA)
Imagine lunch in your hotel is a
complete COMEDY of errors.

○ The Spanish for DINNER is CENA (THENA)
Imagine getting THINNER after eating your dinner.

○ The Spanish for TOBACCO is TABACO (TABAKO)
Imagine a bullfighter filling his pipe with TOBACCO.

○ The Spanish for NEWSPAPER (PEREE ODEEKO)
is PERIÓDICO
Imagine looking at your newspaper PERIODICALLY.

○ The Spanish for NAME is NOMBRE (NOMBRAY)
Imagine asking a policeman for his
name and NUMBER.

○ The Spanish for SOAP is JABÓN (HABON)
Imagine giving a child a piece of soap
and saying 'HAVE ONE.'

O   What is the English for jabón?   _____

O   What is the English for nombre?   _____

O   What is the English for periódico?   _____

O   What is the English for tabaco?   _____

O   What is the English for cena?   _____

O   What is the English for comida?   _____

O   What is the English for desayuno?   _____

O   What is the English for cigarillo?   _____

TURN BACK FOR THE ANSWERS

YOU CAN WRITE YOUR ANSWERS IN, BUT COVER UP THE
LEFT-HAND PAGE BEFORE GIVING YOUR ANSWERS

O   What is the Spanish for soap?   _____

O   What is the Spanish for name?   _____

O   What is the Spanish for newspaper?   _____

O   What is the Spanish for tobacco?   _____

O   What is the Spanish for dinner?   _____

O   What is the Spanish for lunch?   _____

O   What is the Spanish for breakfast?   _____

O   What is the Spanish for cigarette?   _____

TURN BACK FOR THE ANSWERS

LEISURE WORDS

THINK OF EACH IMAGE IN YOUR MIND'S EYE FOR ABOUT TEN SECONDS.

○ The Spanish for PARTY is FIESTA   (FEE ESTA)
   Imagine having a FEAST in the middle of your party.

○ The Spanish for BULLFIGHT is CORRIDA   (KORREEDA)
   Imagine having a bullfight in a CORRIDOR.

○ The Spanish for RIVER is RÍO   (REE O)
   Imagine a famous river, the RIO Grande.

○ The Spanish for MOUNTAIN is MONTAÑA   (MONTANYA)
   Imagine mountains in the American state of MONTANA.

○ The Spanish for STAMP is SELLO   (SELYO)
   Imagine someone who wants to SELL YOU a stamp.

○ The Spanish for ENVELOPE is SOBRE   (SOBRAY)
   Imagine being SOBER enough, just, to stick
   down an envelope.

○ The Spanish for LETTER is CARTA   (KARTA)
   Imagine Ex-President Jimmy CARTER
   reading a letter.

○ The Spanish for BOOK is LIBRO   (LEEBRO)
   Imagine a LIBRARY with books.

YOU CAN WRITE YOUR ANSWERS IN, BUT COVER UP THE
LEFT-HAND PAGE BEFORE GIVING YOUR ANSWERS

○ What is the English for libro?   _____

○ What is the English for carta?   _____

○ What is the English for sobre?   _____

○ What is the English for sello?   _____

○ What is the English for montaña?   _____

○ What is the English for río?   _____

○ What is the English for corrida?   _____

○ What is the English for fiesta?   _____

YOU CAN WRITE YOUR ANSWERS IN

O   What is the Spanish for book?   _____

O   What is the Spanish for letter?   _____

O   What is the Spanish for envelope?   _____

O   What is the Spanish for stamp?   _____

O   What is the Spanish for mountain?   _____

O   What is the Spanish for river?   _____

O   What is the Spanish for bullfight?   _____

O   What is the Spanish for party?   _____

TURN BACK FOR THE ANSWERS

A FINAL TEST

What is the Spanish for

1] RICE...
2] BLOUSE ....
3] TABLE..
4] POTATO ....
5] AMBULANCE ....
6] CUP ....
7] FACE ....
8] MOUTH ....
9] MOTHER ....
10] OIL ....
11] TICKET ....
12] TWO ....
13] DOCTOR ....
14] SEA...
15] ENGINE......................................
16] SORRY ....
17] DOOR...
18] MONDAY ....
19] WHERE.......................................
20] NIGHT ....
21] FRIEND ....
22] NAME ....
23] BULLFIGHT..............................
24] LETTER ....
25] BOOK ....

What is the English for

1] SOPA ....
2] ZAPATO ....
3] CAMA...
4] CARNE..
5] PASTEL ....
6] VENDA ....
7] CAMERERA ....
8] MANO ....
9] MUJER ....
10] TREN ....
11] SEÑORAS......................................
12] ABOGADO ....
13] ARENA..
14] LLAVE ....
15] ADIÓS ....
16] COCINA ....
17] MARTES ....
18] GAMBA...
19] CÚANTO..
20] DÍA ....
21] TARDE ....
22] PAPEL..
23] DESAYUNO...............................
24] PERIÓDICO ....
25] JABÓN ....

THE ANSWERS ARE ON PAGE 76

THE ANSWERS ARE

1] ARROZ	1] SOUP
2] BLUSA	2] SHOE
3] MESA	3] BED
4] PATATA	4] MEAT
5] AMBULANCIA	5] CAKE
6] TAZA	6] BANDAGE
7] CARA	7] WAITRESS
8] BOCA	8] HAND
9] MADRE	9] WIFE
10] ACEITE	10] TRAIN
11] BILLETE	11] LADIES
12] DOS	12] LAWYER
13] MÉDICO	13] SAND
14] MAR	14] KEY
15] MOTOR	15] GOODBYE
16] PERDONE	16] KITCHEN
17] PUERTO	17] TUESDAY
18] LUNES	18] PRAWN
19] DÓNDE	19] HOW MUCH
20] NOCHE	20] DAY
21] AMIGO	21] AFTERNOON
22] NOMBRE	22] PAPER
23] CORRIDA	23] BREAKFAST
24] CARTA	24] NEWSPAPER
25] LIBRE	25] SOAP

Do not worry about spelling. If you had more than 25/50 correct
you have learned 100+ words. 38/50 = 150 words and so on.

IMPORTANT NOTE

This is the end of the course. We hope you have enjoyed it. Of course what you have learned will not make you fluent, but it will help enormously in a large number of situations which you will meet abroad. Don't be afraid to try out what you have learned. Your host will appreciate you making the effort, even if you are sometimes wrong.

The Linkword Method is a very fast method of learning. However, as with any other method of language learning, some of the words will be forgotten unless you go over them from time to time or use them in real life situations. It is strongly recommended that you go over the whole course again a day or two after you have completed it, and then about a month later. Don't worry about forgetting some words. You will be surprised at how quickly you relearn any that you have forgotten when you go over the course again, and just think of all the words you *have* learned.

GLOSSARY

ACCIDENT	– ACCIDENTE	COUGH	– TOS
AFTERNOON	– TARDE	CUP	– TAZA
AMBULANCE	– AMBULANCIA	CUPBOARD	– ARMARIO
ARM	– BRAZO	CURTAIN	– CORTINA
BANDAGE	– VENDA	CUSTOMS	– ADUANA
BANK	– BANCO	DANGER	– PELIGRO
BATH	– BAÑO	DAUGHTER	– HIJA
BATHING		DAY	– DÍA
TRUNKS	– BAÑADOR	DECKCHAIR	– HAMACA
BEACH	– PLAYA	DENTIST	– DENTISTA
BED	– CAMA	DINNER	– CENA
BEDROOM	– DORMITORIO	DOCTOR	– MÉDICO
BEER	– CERVEZA	DOOR	– PUERTA
BILL	– CUENTA	DRAWER	– CAJÓN
BLOOD	– SANGRE	DRESS	– VESTIDO
BLOUSE	– BLUSA	DRIVER	– CONDUCTOR
BOAT	– BARCO	EGG	– HUEVO
BOOK	– LIBRO	ENGINE	– MOTOR
BOTTLE	– BOTELLA	ENTRANCE	– ENTRADA
BOY	– MUCHACHO	ENVELOPE	– SOBRE
BREAD	– PAN	EXHAUST	– ESCAPE
BREAKFAST	– DESAYUNO	EXIT	– SALIDA
BROTHER	– HERMANO	EYE	– OJO
BULLFIGHT	– CORRIDA	FACE	– CARA
BUS	– AUTOBÚS	FAN	– VENTILADOR
CAKE	– PASTEL	FATHER	– PADRE
CAMPING SITE	– CAMPING	FILLET	– FILETE
CAR	– COCHE	FIRE	– FUEGO
CHAIR	– SILLA	FLOOR	– SUELO
CHEESE	– QUESO	FORK	– TENEDOR
CHOP	– CHULETA	FRIEND	– AMIGO
CIGARETTE	– CIGARILLO	GARAGE	– GARAJE
CLAM	– ALMEJA	GARDEN	– JARDIN
CLOCK	– RELOJ	GENTLEMEN	– SEÑORES
COFFEE	– CAFÉ	GIRL	– MUCHACHA
COLD	– FRÍO	GOODBYE	– ADIÓS

HAND	– MANO	OIL	– ACEITE
HAT	– SOMBRERO	ONION	– CEBOLLA
HAVE (I)	– TENGO	ONLY	– SOLAMENTE
HEAT	– CALOR	PAIN	– DOLOR
HELLO	– HOLÁ	PAPER	– PAPEL
HELP	– AYUDA	PARTY	– FIESTA
HOSPITAL	– HOSPITAL	PASSPORT	– PASAPORTE
HOTEL	– HOTEL	PEAR	– PERA
HOUR	– HORA	PETROL	– GASOLINA
HOW	– CÓMO	PICNIC	– MERIENDA
HUSBAND	– MARIDO	PLATE	– PLATO
ILL	– ENFERMO	PLEASE	– POR FAVOR
JACK	– GATO	POLICE	– POLICÍA
KEY	– LLAVE	PORK	– CERDO
KITCHEN	– COCINA	POST OFFICE	– CORREO
KNIFE	– CUCHILLO	POTATO	– PATATA
LADIES	– SEÑORAS	PRAWN	– GAMBA
LAWYER	– ABOGADO	PUNCTURE	– PINCHAZO
LETTER	– CARTA	RESTAURANT	– RESTAURANTE
LETTER BOX	– BUZÓN	RICE	– ARROZ
LOBSTER	– LANGOSTA	RIVER	– RÍO
LUNCH	– COMIDA	ROOM	– HABITACIÓN
MEAT	– CARNE	SAND	– ARENA
MENU	– MENÚ	SAUSAGE	– SALCHICHA
MILK	– LECHE	SEA	– MAR
MINUTE	– MINUTO	SEAT	– ASIENTO
MONTH	– MES	SECOND	– SEGUNDO
MORNING	– MAÑANA	SHELF	– ESTANTE
MOTHER	– MADRE	SHIRT	– CAMISA
MOUNTAIN	– MONTAÑA	SHOE	– ZAPATO
MOUTH	– BOCA	SISTER	– HERMANA
MUSSEL	– MEJILLÓN	SKIN	– PIEL
NAME	– NOMBRE	SKIRT	– FALDA
NEWSPAPER	– PERIÓDICO	SOAP	– JABÓN
NIGHT	– NOCHE	SON	– HIJO
NO	– NO	SORRY	– PERDONE
NOT	– NO	SOUP	– SOPA
NUMBER	– NÚMERO	SPEAK (I)	– HABLO

SQUID	– CALAMAR	**Days of the week**	
STAIRS	– ESCALERA		
STAMP	– SELLO	MONDAY	– LUNES
STEW	– ESTOFADO	TUESDAY	– MARTES
SUGAR	– AZÚCAR	WEDNESDAY	– MIÉRCOLES
SUITCASE	– MALETA	THURSDAY	– JUEVES
SUN	– SOL	FRIDAY	– VIERNES
TABLE	– MESA	SATURDAY	– SÁBADO
TABLECLOTH	– MANTEL	SUNDAY	– DOMINGO
TAKE (I)	– TOMO		
TANK	– DEPÓSITO		
TELEPHONE	– TELÉFONO	**Numbers**	
THANK YOU	– GRACIAS		
THIEF	– LADRÓN	ONE	– UNO
TICKET	– BILLETE	TWO	– DOS
TOBACCO	– TABACO	THREE	– TRES
TOILET	– RETRETE	FOUR	– CUATRO
TOMATO	– TOMATE	FIVE	– CINCO
TRAIN	– TREN	SIX	– SEIS
TROUSERS	– PANTALONES	SEVEN	– SIETE
TYRE	– NEUMÁTICO	EIGHT	– OCHO
VERY	– MUY	NINE	– NUEVE
WAITRESS	– CAMARERA	ZERO	– CERO
WALL	– PARED		
WANT (I)	– QUIERO		
WATER	– AGUA		
WEEK	– SEMANA		
WHEEL	– RUEDA		
WHERE	– DÓNDE		
WHO	– QUIÉN		
WHY	– POR QUÉ		
WIFE	– MUJER		
WINDOW	– VENTANA		
WINE	– VINO		
WRITE (I)	– ESCRIBO		
YEAR	– AÑO		
YES	– SÍ		

LINKWORD SPANISH
by Dr Michael M. Gruneberg

LINKWORD is the language course which teaches you how to remember what you learn as you learn it.

LINKWORD SPANISH is an ideal follow-up to **LINKWORD SPANISH IN A DAY**. In addition to refreshing most of the vocabulary you have already learned, **LINKWORD SPANISH** teaches you an additional extensive vocabulary using the same Linkword method. Furthermore, the **LINKWORD SPANISH** book links the words taught to grammar points in a simple step by step way, and both grammar and vocabulary learning is reinforced by translation exercises which have been carefully designed to maximize speed of learning. After 10–12 hours you will not only have an extensive vocabulary, but the ability to construct sentences using the grammar.

'The most entertaining language system of all:
it works and it's fun'
Guardian

LINKWORD works by association and memory to teach vocabulary <u>and</u> <u>grammar</u> in a simple step by step way. If you are a business person or holidaymaker and want to take your Spanish to a higher level, if you are studying Spanish at school or if you learned Spanish at school and are now rusty – whatever your reasons – **LINKWORD SPANISH** will help you improve fast and cope more confidently.

0 552 13055 9

LINKWORD
LANGUAGE SYSTEM
by Dr Michael M. Gruneberg

LINKWORD is the language course which teaches you how to remember what you learn as you learn it. LINKWORD is the fastest, the easiest, the most enjoyable way to learn a language and is ideal for holidays, business travel and schoolwork!

FOR DETAILS OF HOW TO ORDER AND MORE INFORMATION ABOUT LINKWORD TURN OVER THIS PAGE

LINKWORD LANGUAGE SYSTEM BOOKS, AUDIO TAPES AND BOOK AND TAPE PACKS AVAILABLE FROM CORGI BOOKS

THE PRICES SHOWN BELOW WERE CORRECT AT THE TIME OF GOING TO PRESS. HOWEVER TRANSWORLD PUBLISHERS RESERVE THE RIGHT TO SHOW NEW RETAIL PRICES ON COVERS WHICH MAY DIFFER FROM THOSE PREVIOUSLY ADVERTISED IN THE TEXT OR ELSEWHERE.

☐	14246 8	LINKWORD FRENCH IN A DAY	£3.99
☐	13053 2	LINKWORD LANGUAGE COURSE: FRENCH	£4.99
☐	13916 5	LINKWORD LANGUAGE COURSE: FURTHER FRENCH	£4.99
☐	13054 0	LINKWORD LANGUAGE COURSE: GERMAN	£4.99
☐	14247 6	LINKWORD SPANISH IN A DAY	£3.99
☐	13055 9	LINKWORD LANGUAGE COURSE: SPANISH	£4.99
☐	13056 7	LINKWORD LANGUAGE COURSE: ITALIAN	£4.99
☐	13907 6	LINKWORD LANGUAGE COURSE: GREEK	£4.99
☐	13906 8	LINKWORD LANGUAGE COURSE: PORTUGUESE	£4.99
☐	13225 X	LINKWORD AUDIO TAPE: FRENCH	£6.95*
☐	14062 7	LINKWORD AUDIO TAPE: FURTHER FRENCH	£6.95*
☐	13226 8	LINKWORD AUDIO TAPE: GERMAN	£6.95*
☐	13227 6	LINKWORD AUDIO TAPE: SPANISH	£6.95*
☐	13228 4	LINKWORD AUDIO TAPE: ITALIAN	£6.95*
☐	13955 6	LINKWORD AUDIO TAPE: GREEK	£6.95*
☐	13966 1	LINKWORD AUDIO TAPE: PORTUGUESE	£6.95*
☐	00500 2	LINKWORD BOOK AND TAPE PACK: FRENCH	£11.99*
☐	00370 0	LINKWORD BOOK AND TAPE PACK: GERMAN	£11.99*
☐	00501 0	LINKWORD BOOK AND TAPE PACK: SPANISH	£11.99*

*inclusive of VAT

All Corgi/Bantam Books are available at your bookshop or newsagent, or can be ordered from the following address:
Corgi/Bantam Books
Cash Sales Department
PO Box 11, Falmouth, Cornwall TR10 9EN
UK and BFPO customers please send a cheque or postal order (no currency) and allow £1.00 for postage and packing for the first book plus 50p for the second book and 30p for each additional book to a maximum charge of £3.00 (7 books plus).
Overseas customers, including Eire, please allow £2.00 for postage and packing for the first book plus £1.00 for the second book and 50p for each subsequent title ordered.

NAME (Block letters) ....

ADDRESS ....

....